I0022010

CYBERSECURITY

and

HACKING

for Beginners

The Essential Guide to Mastering Computer Network Security and Learning all the Defensive Actions to Protect Yourself from Network Dangers, Including the Basics of Kali Linux

By

Robert M. Huss

Robert M. Huss
Cybersecurity and Hacking

© **Copyright 2022 by Robert M. Huss - All rights reserved.**

No part of this guide may be reproduced in any form without permission in writing from the publisher except in the case of brief quotations embodied in critical articles or reviews.

Legal & Disclaimer

The information contained in this book and its contents are not designed to replace any form of professional advice; and it is not intended to replace the need for advice or other independent services as may be required. The content and information in this book have been provided for educational and entertainment purposes only.

The content and information contained in this book have been compiled from sources believed to be reliable and cared for to the best of the author's knowledge, information and beliefs. However, the author cannot guarantee its accuracy and validity and cannot be held responsible for any errors and/or omissions. In addition, changes are periodically made to this book as and when necessary. Where appropriate and/or necessary, you should consult a professional before using any of the remedies, techniques or information suggested in this book.

By using the contents and information contained in this book, you agree to indemnify the Author from and against any damages, costs and expenses, including any legal fees potentially arising from the application of any of the information provided in this book. This disclaimer applies to any loss, damage or injury caused by the use and application, either directly or indirectly, of any advice or information presented, whether for breach of contract, tort, negligence, personal injury, criminal intent or any other cause of action.

You agree to accept all risks associated with the use of the information presented in this book.

You agree that by continuing to read this book, where appropriate and/or necessary, you must consult a professional before using any of the suggested remedies, techniques or information in this book.

Table of Contents

CYBERSECURITY 5

INTRODUCTION.. 7

CHAPTER 1   Creation, Use and Management of Passwords 9

How to use passwords.. 9

Choosing your password 11

Password creation tools.. 12

How to manage your passwords 14

How to keep your passwords.. 17

CHAPTER 2   How to Prevent Risks from Infected Emails......21

Attention to phishing 21

Warnings to prevention... 22

Protective tools 23

CHAPTER 3   Avoid Downloading Software or Apps from
Unreliable Sources..25

CHAPTER 4   Making Updates 27

Types of updates 28

CHAPTER 5   Safely Surfing on Internet.......................... 31

Free Wi-Fi networks.. 32

How to protect oneself 34

Use a firewall to monitor activity 35

CHAPTER 6   How to Protect Oneself from External Devices 37

In case of theft or loss of the hardware device.......................... 38

CHAPTER 7   How to Delete Viruses 41

Eliminate the virus from your smartphone 41

Deleting the virus from your computer....................................... 45

How to manually delete viruses from your computer 49

Glossary 57

HACKING 63

DEFINITIONS..65

CHAPTER 1   Types of Hacking......................................67

CHAPTER 2   The Path of a Hacker..............................71

What is a hacker?.. 71

How to become a Hacker... 72

Which are the requirements..73

CHAPTER 3   The Hacking Process...............................75

Gathering information 75

Scanning... 76

Getting Access 77

Maintaining access.. 77

What is Ethical Hacking? 79

CHAPTER 4   Installing and Using Kali Linux 81

What is Kali Linux?.. 81

Features of Kali Linux 82

How to install Kali Linux 86

Minimum requirements for various versions of Kali Linux 86

Installation on a USB key 88

Installation on a PC..94

How to set up Kali Linux on Windows 10...............................99

Working with Kali Linux 102

CHAPTER 5   How to Scan the Network and Servers 105

Scanning a network with Nmap 105

Scanning with Hping3 107

CHAPTER 6   How to Hack a PC and How to Protect Yourself111

Tools for hacking the PC 111

How to protect your PC 113

CYBERSECURITY

By

Robert M. Huss

Robert M. Huss
Cybersecurity and Hacking

INTRODUCTION

Computer networking is an important part of our lives at work, at school and even at home, which is why many people try to figure out how to protect their professional and personal information. As you continue to read, you will discover the importance of protecting our computers/smartphones from possible attacks and information theft. The Internet is not only virtual but what we do every day on the network (bank transfers, purchases etc. ...) is real

Information Security can be defined as the set of measures to ensure user authentication and confidentiality of information and services managed or delivered digitally.

This practice consists in defending computers, servers and mobile devices from dangerous attacks. It is also called electronic information security.

The threats that cyber security seeks to counter are threefold in nature:

1. Cybercrime, when individuals attack systems for financial gain.

2. Cyber war, which concerns the collection of information for political purposes.

3. Cyber-terrorism, intent on undermining computer systems to unleash panic or terror.

The most common methods used by crackers to control computers are:

- Viruses and worms can self-replicate and damage files or systems

- Spyware and Trojans are often used to stealthily collect data. The average user generally comes into contact with malicious codes through unwanted email attachments or through downloading programs that appear legitimate but actually carry malware with them.

CHAPTER 1   Creation, Use and Management of Passwords

How to use passwords

The password or access key is, in computer science or cryptography, a series of alphanumeric characters and special signs used to access a computer resource (Internet connection, email, networks, computers, ATMs, programs, etc...). With a password and user name, the identity of a person is verified, allowing access to various types of IT services. The password is also used to carry out encryption operations.

Protecting our computer data with a password is of paramount importance to avoid unpleasant consequences that could result from unauthorized access by external individuals (hackers).

The consequences can range from unpleasant annoyances to real corporate disasters. For example, if a co-worker discovers your password and wants to cause damage to the company using your PC, the blame for everything will be yours because you have a duty to keep your passwords.

If your email password is discovered, the intruder may use your email address to send computer viruses or take criminal action on your behalf.

It is very difficult to identify the person responsible for the criminal operations after the act has been carried out, because he can operate from anywhere without the need for physical access to your computer.

A statistical survey has shown that the most commonly used passwords in the USA are as follows:

123456	password	12345	12345678	qwerty
123456789	1234	baseball	1234567	abc123
111111	iloveyou	sunshine	princes	admin
welcome	666666	football	123123	monkey
654321	!@#$%^&*	charlie	aa123456	donald

The cracker, i.e. the hacker with illicit intentions, can discover your simple passwords in a few days, using special programs capable of automatically trying even a thousand passwords per second. Therefore, if a cracker decides to discover your password, you will be defenseless.

If the cracker decides to launch a "brute force attack" and with the use of technical specifications, it can shorten the access time by a lot.

Choosing your password

When choosing your password it is important to avoid common words and make sure, you choose unusual terms. Avoid proper names (children, parents, and spouses), team names, cities, movies, artists, etc.

The most effective way to choose a good password is to use an automatic generator that creates unusual and therefore unique character sequences.

These passwords are usually difficult to remember, but the generator has a system for storing the generated passwords. In this case, you only need to choose a password that allows you to activate the generator and then access the other passwords.

To choose the only password to keep in mind, we recommend two approaches.

1. Choose 4/5 words and merge them together. They should not be famous sentences but different words joined together without giving a logical sense

2. Choose a verse from a song or poem and use only a few letters from each word.

You can use multiple techniques in combination.

Password creation tools

F-Secure

F-Secure is a program that can generate complex passwords for each type of service, store them and associate them to email addresses, pin codes, credit card credentials and current accounts.

This program uses the AES-256 encryption system. In addition, the main encryption key is obtained from your master password through a complex algorithm that makes it almost impossible for crackers to detect it.

Last Pass and its installation

Last Pass can be conveniently used through the browser thanks to its official extensions to create robust and secure passwords in a matter of seconds. After downloading the software from the official website, proceed with the installation of the extension according to the procedure provided by your browser. Once you have installed the extension in your browser, you will need to create an account to use the service.

Enter your email address, check "I agree to the LastPass Terms and Privacy Policy" and click on the "Create an account" button.

Fill out the form, enter your master password and click on "next" to complete the registration.

Once you have registered, you will be able to generate your own passwords.

Click on the Lapses icon and "generate secure password".

Set the various options, such as password length, upper/lower case letters, digits, special characters or avoid ambiguous characters.

Once you have created your password, click the "use password" button.

Last Pass synchronizes passwords on all devices associated with the same account and is available as a mobile application.

There are other software or applications that you can use as

- 1Password
- PassworG
- Random Password Generator
- Password Creator
- Norton Password Generator
- RoboForm Password Generator

How to manage your passwords

The advice is to use a different password for each service you use (email account, home banking, credit cards, etc.). If you use a single password for all services, you will be more vulnerable.

In fact, the security system of any normal website (ex. Badoo) where you register is definitely more vulnerable than the security system of your bank. So if you use the same password, it is more likely that a cracker will be able to penetrate the database of users of the well-known online service and can then try to get into more appetizing services.

In the past years, crackers have stolen the access data of millions of users on LinkedIn, Yahoo, Adobe, selling those credentials on the dark web.

There are websites that allow you to check if your data are part of those stolen in hacking episodes.

A website that you can use to check if your passwords have been stolen in some hacking episode is haveinbeenpwned.com.

If a cracker thinks he can make a lot of money by logging into your account, he can invest time and resources in finding your password.

He can put a "botnet" to work, that is a network of computers under his control thanks to a malware, which generates thousands of passwords, until he finds the right one. In this way, the shortest passwords (8/10 words) can be decrypted in a few months.

To make your computer system more secure, you should change your passwords.

This way, a new door to open will always be presented to the hypothetical thief.

It is necessary to determine how often passwords should be changed. A too thin change gives the cracker time to decode the password. Changing passwords too often exposes the cracker to the risk of forgetting them.

The password change used by companies is usually every three months. Everything depends on the data to be protected.

If it is simple accounting data or similar, the frequency of change can be greater than three months.

If, on the other hand, the data is more attractive to crime (trade secrets, access to bank accounts), then the exchange rate will certainly be less than three months.

Do not use the same passwords in your company as for personal profiles.

A very valid and effective countermeasure is the double level authentication.

Two-factor authentication performs two controls to give access. The server that receives our access request can send us on the mobile phone a code to be entered in the second level of verification to confirm access and confirm that it is we at the keyboard.

How to keep your passwords

Generally, there is a total superficiality on the part of employees of a company in storing passwords to access their terminal. Often passwords are transcribed into a post-it attacked at best under the computer keyboard.

In theory, employees should only frequent a company's offices, but it is possible for other people to come in as messengers, technicians to repair failures in air conditioning systems or cleaners, or more.

"Social engineering" is often used by hackers to steal passwords to access the company network.

Hackers can sneak into offices, for example as messengers, and use the access data.

Another "social engineering" technique used by hackers is to obtain information by making a false phone call or sending false e-mails. In general, these techniques do not arouse particular suspicion in the case of large organizations. In fact, in these cases, the malevolent hacker can pass himself off as a bank employee who has to do accounting checks.

Passwords that are not kept properly can be stolen not only by malevolent external individuals, but also by your colleagues who want to create damage to the company. Also in this case, if the malicious colleague creates damage to the company from your computer, the responsibility is yours because you have not done everything possible to prevent other people from becoming aware of your access data.

Also keeping all your passwords in a file is a lack of custody because the evil intent can copy without your knowledge the above file in a USB and search for what it needs in a second momentum and calmly.

The best solution to store passwords is to use a password manager tool such as Key F-Secure Key. It is based on encrypting the master password by subjecting it to a complex mathematical function and adding an authentication code based on 256-bit hashes, by entering causal data.

Other tools:

Google Smart Lock: This tool allows you to save passwords to the cloud and synchronize them on various devices. In this way, it allows you to use your passwords whenever you access the Internet via Google Chrome or from your Android device. To activate Smart Lock, scroll to the right and go to "Security" to activate "vases" on "settings", then on Google and Google accounts. Scroll to "how to access other sites" and click on "saved passwords". Here you can decide whether to enable or disable "Ask to save passwords".

If you want to set this option on your PC, go to your profile and click on "password". Now decide whether to enable or disable the "Ask to save passwords" option.

iCloud Keyring: This is an Apple tool. To activate, go to "Settings" and click on your name and press "iCloud". On the next screen click on "keychain" and turn the switch on.

If you want to set up the Keychain on your Mac, go to the top left and click on the Apple logo. Select the "System Preferences" option and check the "Keychain" box.

Robert M. Huss
Cybersecurity and Hacking

CHAPTER 2 How to Prevent Risks from Infected Emails

Email control is one of the first actions that each employee takes every morning when they arrive at the office. The worst threats can reach our computer from e-mail. Usually, your email provider eliminates junk mail (spam), such as advertisements and emails that contain malware. However, every now and then some of them manage to get to our computer.

Attention to phishing

Phishing is one of the oldest and most effective techniques used by crackers to hack computer systems.

Opening an email that contains a virus can cause significant damage to your business.

For example, an email with a PDF attachment may arrive; perhaps in the email trap it is indicated to open the attachment for more details. When the attachment is opened, the hard disk is moved and in a few seconds all

21

our documents are encrypted and a screen appears that warns us of the incident and that to get our documents back we have to pay a ransom. In the meantime, the virus reaches the server and infects the entire company network. This type of virus is called Ransomware. This described is the worst-case scenario that can arise.

Other emails may contain Trojan viruses of various types such as keyloggers. This virus records everything you type on your computer's keyboard and transmits it to hackers who then come into possession of accounts and passwords.

Not all infected emails contain attachments, but they may contain links that activate the virus at the same time as you click on the link.

Warnings to prevention

The first thing to do is to have a good anti-spam system. This is usually offered free of charge by your e-mail provider. In case you want to improve your security, providers offer paid anti-spam systems that have advanced security features.

Let us give you some simple tips in case suspicious emails arrive:

- Do not respond to emails that deceptively seem to come from banks, where you are asked to confirm your credentials. The banks know your data and in case of confirmation, they will invite you to go physically to the bank.
- Move the cursor over the sender's address and you will see that the address changes. It is no longer the address of the known bank or courier.
- Passing the cursor over the link contained within the suspicious email will show you that the web address is not what appears in the email.
- Be wary of any emails that tell you they are winners or heirs of anything. It sounds absurd, but these types of emails are still being sent so it means that someone is still falling for them.

Protective tools

In most cases, it is sufficient to leave the protections offered by the operating system active: the antivirus "Windows Defender" on Microsoft operating systems, the protection system "Gatekeeper" on Macs and "Google Play Protect" on Android.

A good email protection system is the one offered by F-Secure, "E-mail and Server Security", which protects your company's servers, email and cloud systems. This tool is based on behavior analysis and the use of whitelists and blacklists.

Installing an anti-virus can guarantee the security of your emails. You can also add anti-malware for a higher level of security. These programs can be run on an occasional basis to detect any running threats that are well hidden and/or invisible to the antivirus.

One of the most powerful and effective malware around is Malwarebyte. You can find it free on the Internet.

CHAPTER 3   Avoid Downloading Software or Apps from Unreliable Sources

Downloading and installing pirated software is prohibited by law, but this is not a good deterrent given the huge amount of software that is downloaded.

Initially, such software was contained in the P2P circuits (the famous Torrent and eMule). Today we also find them in file sharing circuits (heirs of Rapidshare).

Generally, the virus is hidden in the program that generates the fake serial number to activate the main program. When the "keygen" is started, it asks permission to make changes to the system. At this point, it can do whatever it wants. It can install a Keylogger and at worst a Ransomware.

Even the installation of legal software does not protect you from the risks.

Not all Apps downloaded from Play store are what they seem. In particular, clones of famous apps and games are often traps. These clones are often available on the platform even before the official App came out.

The most vulnerable devices are mobile ones like smartphones and tablets. In particular, those that use

Android because the controls of the official store are not very thorough and often Google removes only afterwards the infected Apps.

You can check the reliability of programs that are downloaded from the store with some online services such as VirusTotal, the online antivirus that uses 68 different antivirus engines to check any type of file (or Internet address). All this is completely free and without any registration.

WOT is an online service that allows you to analyze the reliability of websites through the opinions and reviews of users.

In the case of a corporate network, the ideal solution is the implementation of precise corporate policies regarding the software on the various devices. In addition, it is advisable that user accounts are not "administrator" type. Position riserve for IT staff.

We always recommend the presence of an anti-virus such as "Client Security" and "Protection service for Business", able to scan files and provide greater security, blocking software that tries to perform dangerous operations.

CHAPTER 4   Making Updates

Programming a software or an App is such a broad process that it is almost impossible to predict all possible defects.

All software or operating systems when they are programmed contain critical points, i.e. defects, which can be exploited by crackers to fit into other people's computers or computer networks and install malicious programs without the user noticing anything.

In the computer world, there is a continuous war that sees on the one hand crackers trying to discover the critical points in software, operated systems and Apps, to exploit them to their advantage, usually illegal. On the other hand, there are hackers who test programs to improve them, detect defects and communicate them to manufacturers so that they can update software by eliminating critical points.

When a cracker discovers a "critical point", which in jargon is called "zero day", he tries to prepare an "exploit".

The exploit allows you to enter the PC, becoming its administrator.

Once inside the PC, the cracker can read the data, modify or delete the files, steal credentials or install a keylogger.

After the first infections have spread, the software manufacturer intervenes by eliminating the critical points and updating the program.

Subsequently, the update alert is sent to all users.

Here is the importance of performing updates.

Types of updates

In general, there are two types of updates.

Major update: These updates are used to improve performance and introduce new features. Before making such updates, you will need to check your computer for compatibility. In other words, features that are more powerful may be required. For example, if the operating system is affected by such updates, a more powerful memory or processor may be required. In this case, if this involves a company network, you will first need to analyze the devices and then update them if necessary. In fact, if the devices are not adequate, the update could cause a malfunction of the network.

Minor update: these updates are used to fix errors, bugs or vulnerabilities. These updates are issued without notice and must be installed immediately. In Apps, automatic availability notifications are usually activated for these types of updates.

In the case of version updates, one unit increases the serial number of the software. Example, Windows 7 to Windows 8.

In the case of limited changes or improvements from the previous version, the first decimal place of the serial number is increased. Example, Windows 8 to Windows 8.1.

If the update concerns security, then the second decimal place is increased. Example, Windows 8.1.2.

If the security management concerns a computer network, we recommend using a centralized management system such as "Software Updater" included in "Protection Service for Business" and "Premium Business Suite" of F-Secure.

Smartphone

Upgrading your smartphone means protecting yourself from all possible dangers. Not only Google, but also smartphone manufacturers are constantly updating their devices. Moreover, the reason is always the same: Updates correct leaks and protect against new threats. There is no reason to refuse to download updates. If you think that the applications in the official markets are completely safe, you are wrong. Apps can contain infected links and because of our superficiality, we download apps and open links even if they come from unknown sources.

CHAPTER 5   Safely Surfing on Internet

Surfing the Internet increases the likelihood of being affected by malware simply by visiting a website. The most dangerous sites are not those that everyone can think of, such as online gaming sites or porn sites. In fact, these sites are very vigilant in ensuring the safety of their users from possible threats such as malware.

Malware is more likely to be contracted on airline, newspaper, food or insurance sites. These sites are more attractive to crackers because they generate high traffic. Typically, the cracker attacks the vulnerabilities of browsers or their plug-ins with Javascript to download and install their malware. Another method used by crackers is to download an infected file by passing it through a video codec, without which it is not possible to see a certain movie.

In some cases, malware can be contained within advertising banners.

Finally, crackers can create real web sites traps, by conveying the bad guys with messages on Facebook inviting them to visit these web sites, but using an abbreviated address that does not allow you to understand where you are going. Once the cracker can get the malware installed, he is free to do what he wants.

To defend yourself from possible attacks on the web you need to keep your browser and plug-ins up to date. Better still if the plug-ins are activated only on demand.

To block the execution of Javascript programs and advertising banners, it is advisable to install a "scriptblocker" in the first case, and an "adblocker" in the second case.

We can compile a "whitelist" and insert all the sites we trust.

A good antivirus combined with a good anti-malware guarantee the protection of incoming files and the control of internet traffic to block access to dangerous sites.

Client Security can control and block access to websites and protect against executable files.

Free Wi-Fi networks

The hunting grounds preferred by crackers are free Wi-Fi networks, i.e. not for a fee.

Free Wi-Fi networks are easy to access and there is no risk of being identified.

In fact, in these networks, the cracker can perform a MitM attack "Man in the middle". It consists of letting the bad person think that he is connected to the Wi-Fi, while in reality its data flow passes through the cracker's computer. In turn, the cracker, after checking and recording this data, passes it on to the hotspot, making the person who happened to be connected directly to the Wi-Fi network believe he is.

The worst case is when the hotspot is under the control of the cracker or even was created by it to attack all those who will connect. In this case, the cracker has control of the router. A trap of this kind is called a "honeypot".

There are also hardware devices capable of intercepting devices that try to connect to the free Wi-Fi network, and that respond to the connection attempt by pretending to be the desired network.

Finally, it is possible that they will connect to the network computers already infected with malware and will try to transmit the virus to all other connected terminals.

How to protect oneself

As a first step, it is advisable to avoid, while connected to a public Wi-Fi network, operations of transfer of sensitive data or information access to various services.

The use of a VPN system can be a good tool to ensure security when connecting via public networks.

The VPN encrypts the data exchanged during the connection, making it unusable by crackers. In addition, the VPN should also be used for Https connections because these can be easily intercepted and decoded.

Other preventive actions to be taken are:

- Disabling file sharing
- Disable the automatic connection to free Wi-Fi networks, which is usually set as active on the various terminals.

All these prevention measures are necessary because there is no way of knowing whether a public Wi-Fi network is secure or not.

Use a firewall to monitor activity

A firewall is a protection system, software or hardware, that prevents unauthorized access by protecting two different networks.

The operating systems, Windows and macOS have integrated a firewall that is active by default (and that can be deactivated if necessary). But it is also possible to download third-party firewalls such as the so-called Windows Firewall Control (for Windows) and Little Snitch (for macOS), which extend the functionality of the default firewall on your computer and allow you to monitor network activities even more easily.

Robert M. Huss
Cybersecurity and Hacking

CHAPTER 6 How to Protect Oneself from External Devices

External components, such as USB sticks and CDs, are susceptible to infection.

Years ago, Microsoft inserted a file called "Autorun.inf" to simplify the installation of software by non-experts.

Therefore, when you insert a component external to your computer, Windows checks if it contains the "Autorun.inf" file and runs it.

Therefore, the cracker who wants to enter a computer can put the infected file in autorun and hide it on a USB stick. As soon as the USB stick is inserted into the computer, it starts the file in autorun and infects the computer.

Tablets and smartphones can also be infected through USB ports.

When you charge your smartphone by connecting it to a USB port, for example in airports, hotels or public places, a virus may infect you.

In theory, these USB ports should be connected to simple power transformers. There have been reports that behind these simple USB power ports were real controllers that could connect to the device and steal data from it.

Such an operation requires well-organized groups of crackers.

To prevent a possible USB infection, it is advisable to disable autorun on your computer by changing the settings on the "registry". If you are not able to handle the "registry", you should consult an expert.

F-Secure's "security for mobile" software is designed to prevent infections from USB sticks.

To prevent such infections on smartphones, we recommend using a "USB condom". That is, a USB extension cable in which the cables for the data connection have been removed, leaving only those for power supply. In this way, there is no possibility of starting a data connection.

In case of theft or loss of the hardware device

To protect yourself against the physical theft of the computer used to access our sensitive data, it is advisable to enter robust passwords to access the system.

However, this does not completely protect us from the theft of our sensitive data on your computer. Because the intentional evil can detach the hard disk from the computer and install it on another computer. This way you will have the possibility to access the data.

It is advisable to use full disk encryption. This way, even if you install the hard disk on another computer, the data will be unreadable without the access key.

The side effect would be not to recover your data if your computer fails. That is why it is always advisable to back up your data.

To increase security, you can enter specific software that will erase all data in the event of theft or loss.

To protect your smartphone from theft or loss, software has been installed to email you the location of your device and a photo of who is using it.

In addition, on both Apple and Android, applications have been introduced such as "find my smartphone," that allows you to locate where it is.

Robert M. Huss
Cybersecurity and Hacking

CHAPTER 7   How to Delete Viruses

If you suspect that, a virus has infected your computer or phone but do not know how to verify it and possibly how to solve the problem, the actions to be taken are as follows.

Eliminate the virus from your smartphone

Android System

Android devices do not need to have an antivirus, as there are settings that automatically block the installation of unknown applications that could harm the device.

To check this, go to "settings", then click on "security" and check if the entry "unknown sources is disabled.

If you have an Android 8 or later, go to "Settings" then "Apps and Notifications" > "Advanced" > "Special App Access" > "Install Unknown Apps".

Make sure that all apps in the list are marked "not allowed". If not, move the stick from left to right.

I recommend that you do not root your Android device to get all the permissions. This practice can make your Android device vulnerable and expose it to serious dangers, as it is often used to circumvent the protection systems of some Apps.

Google Play Protect is a free system for all Android systems, which regularly scans all the Apps in the Play Store and those installed on your device to verify their security.

To verify that this service is active, go to the Play Store and from the menu at the top left, select Play Protector. Make sure that the "Search for security threats" box next to it is active. You can also select the next item, "Enhance malicious app detection", for added security.

To identify and resolve the possible problem with your smartphone, Android allows you to enter Safe Mode.

There is no standard procedure. Here are two procedures.

Procedure 1: Press and hold the physical power off/lock screen button on your Android device. When the options appear, hold down the "power off" option until the "restart in safe mode" option appears and press "OK".

Procedure 2: When turning your mobile phone on or off, as soon as the manufacturer's logo for your device appears, press and hold the Volume Down key (or Home key). "Safe Mode" will appear.

When in Safe Mode, check the list of installed Apps and see if there are any that, you think you have not installed. Be careful because some apps you do not know may be useful for your operating system. If you do not have root permissions, it is better because you will not be able to uninstall system Apps.

If you have found the malicious app, tap on it and then tap on uninstall.

If you cannot remove an App, it probably has permission to administer your device, so you will first have to remove that permission and then uninstall it.

To remove this permission, go to Settings > Security > Device Administrators. Once you have found the malicious App, remove the check mark.

To exit Safe Mode, restart your phone.

If you cannot delete the virus following the procedure described above, it is advisable to do a **factory reset**.

The **factory reset** allows you to reset your phone to the state it was in when you purchased it. All data and applications installed after purchase will be deleted. Therefore, it is important that you make a backup of your device's files to avoid losing anything.

To start this process, go to Settings > Backup & Restore > Factory Data Recovery.

If you have an Android 8 go to Settings > System > Reset Options > Delete all data.

iOS System

The operating system of Apple devices is safe and the risk of getting into a virus is low. It all depends on how you use your device; jailbreaking and installing Apps from unofficial sources is always not recommended.

The jailbreak allows you to circumvent the restrictions imposed by Apple on its iOS operating system.

This practice makes the system vulnerable and can cause damage to the device, leading to the installation of malware.

Deleting the virus from your computer

We assume that the best way to defend ourselves against possible attacks is through prevention.

Installing a good anti-virus is definitely the best prevention action.

Bitdefender Free is a free anti-virus that defends against all aspects of the system: files opened and downloaded from the Internet, communications on instant messaging services, items downloaded via P2P and much more.

After downloading the installation package called "Antivirus_Free_Edition.exe", click the Yes button and select the language from the drop-down menu.

To get the free version of Bitdefender Free you need to register on MyBitdefender, otherwise the copy of the program will expire after 30 days of trial.

To start a full PC scan, right-click on the newly installed program icon and select "full scan".

At the end of the procedure, you will be shown a report that indicates all the files scanned, any threats detected and the actions taken.

You can also scan individual files by dragging them directly onto the Bitdefender icon.

Another good free antivirus is Avira free antivirus. It has the same functions as Bitdefender, but is heavier.

Using "self-start" antivirus

In some cases, it is not possible to delete the virus from the computer with the use of classic antivirus. It is necessary to intervene in a forced manner. That is, it is necessary to intervene before the computer, during the start-up phase, starts the operating system. This is possible with ad hoc tools, downloaded and installed on a CD or USB stick.

The first tool I recommend is **Bitdefender Recuse CD**.

This tool requires an active connection to the Internet, so it can update the list of viruses and detect the latest threats

To download the program go to the website and click on "To create a Bitdefender Rescue CD on a CD/DVD you need the ISO image which care be downloaded from here".

Then choose whether to burn the antivirus to a CD/DVD or copy it to a USB stick.

If you decide to burn it to a CD, then use any burning program.

If you decide to copy it to a USB stick, then you can download the free software provided by Bitdefender itself. Click on "Stickifier executable".

Select the ISO image of the antivirus and then the stick to copy the files to.

To scan your computer, insert the USB stick (or CD).

When the antivirus screen appears, click Start the Bitdefender Rescue CD to start Bitdefender Rescue CD.

If the screen does not appear, then you will need to make a change to your BIOS.

Enter the BIOS and set the CD/DVD drive or USB port as the primary boot drive.

In the window with the software license agreement check next to "By checking this box I agree to the license agreement lists above" and click on "Continue".

The list of viruses will be updated and to start a scan click first on "Scan now" and then on "Star".

Another self-starting antivirus **Kaspersky Rescue Disk.**

Download the program from the website, then click on "Download & Info", and then on the "Distribute" button.

Choose whether to download the antivirus to CD or USB stick.

Restart the system and boot from the newly created media.

Press any key when the message "Press any key to enter the menu" appears.

Kaspersky will start automatically.

Press button 1 and select "Kaspersky Rescue Disk Graphic Mode".

Click on "My update center" and then "Start" to start updating your antivirus definitions.

Before starting a full system scan, you must make sure that you have selected the items "Disk boot sectors", "Hidden startup objects" and "C" on the Object scans tab.

Press the "Start objects scan" button to start the scan.

There are some types of Malware or Adware that escape antivirus control.

Usually, these are less aggressive threats than viruses, but still annoying. For example, those who install toolbars and redirect navigation to sites full of advertising messages.

To combat these types of malware, it is advisable to install free software such as "Adwcleaner" and "Malwarebytes".

How to manually delete viruses from your computer

To manually delete viruses from your computer, you need to have an advanced knowledge of your computer and the operation of your operating system.

In fact, you need to identify the infected file and delete it or uninstall the program that contains that file.

If this operation is not done in an exact manner, it can compromise the operation of the computer and in the worst case, it will be necessary to start a formatting of the computer with the consequence of losing all the data present in it.

On Pc

If you are using Windows, the first thing to do is to create a restore point, to be used if the stability of the operating system is compromised.

Simultaneously press the Ctrl+Shift+Esc keys and start the "Task Manager".

Click on "more details" and then on the "processes" tab.

Check the list of running processes and if you notice something that you do not like, note it down and search on Google.

If you find that, the running process is a virus, right-click on the suspicious process and select "Open file path".

Connect to the VirusTotal website and drag the suspicious file to the website pane.

VirusTotal will analyze the suspicious file and if you are infected, you must delete it.

To delete the infected file, go to the "Processes" tab, right-click on the name of the infected file, select "End Processes

Tree / End Activity Tree" from the menu and confirm by clicking the "Yes" button.

If the infected file belongs to a program, go to Control Panel > Programs and Features > Uninstall a program. Select the program and click on "Uninstall".

You can also delete the infected file by right-clicking on the file and holding down the "Shift" key select "delete" and press "Yes".

This procedure may affect the functioning of the operating system or leave virus residues invisible.

Once you have manually deleted the virus, restart your computer and check the programs that start when you start Windows.

If you find the program again, you must remove it from the startup list.

If you have Windows 10, go to "Task Manager", click on "Start" and locate the file, right click on the file and select "Disable".

If you have previous versions of Windows, press Win+R at the same time. A panel will appear where you can type the command "msconfig", press "Enter" and click on the Start tab. One. Once you have identified the infected program, remove the check mark, click on OK and then on Restart to perform an immediate restart of the computer.

As a last check to verify that the infected file has been completely deleted, go and check the extensions of the browsers you use.

Access the settings of the browser you are using:

- **Chrome**, click on the button (⋮) located at the top right, go to the Other Tools > Extensions menu.
- **Firefox**, click on the ☰ button in the upper right corner, then on "Add-ons" and choose "Extensions" from the left sidebar.
- **Microsoft Edge**, press the button (...) and click on the "Extensions" item from the menu that opens.

If an error message such as "Access denied" or "Cannot execute" appears during virus deletion, you must start the PC in "Safe Mode" and delete the virus from this mode.

Once you have permanently deleted the virus from your PC, you must take the necessary precautions so that this does not happen again.

- Do not download programs from unknown and suspicious sites, attachments received via email, social networks.
- Always keep your operating system up to date.
- Install a good solution.
- Never disable operating system or antivirus protections.

Note: If you still experience a computer malfunction then the virus is still present. In this case, you would need to intervene on the "Registry". Quite a complicated and delicate operation. It is therefore advisable to install an anti-virus that performs all the necessary operations in complete safety.

On Mac

If you are using a Mac, the probability of finding an infection is very low.

However, should your Mac be infected, the first thing to do is to check all the software currently running with the Mac Activity Monitoring utility.

Click on the Go > Finder Utility menu and launch the Activity Monitoring tool.

Carefully observe all running processes and identify suspicious ones.

Search Google to make sure it is a threat.

In case you have confirmation that it is a virus, go back to the Activity Monitoring window and click on the infected process, then on the button(s) at the top and finally twice on the Exit button. This will immediately deactivate the harmful activity.

To permanently delete the virus, go to the Applications folder of your Mac, identify the "offending" program, right-click on the relevant file and select the Move to Trash item and then "Empty Trash".

As a last check to make sure that the virus has been completely deleted, go and check the Safari browser extensions.

Go to the Safari > Preferences menu, go to the "Extensions" tab, select the infected extension and click on "Uninstall".

If you cannot delete the virus and its extensions in your browser then you will need to start your Mac in "Safe Mode" and delete the virus from this mode.

To start the Mac in "Safe Mode", press and hold the Shift key while restarting the computer.

When the Apple logo appears and you see the login window, release the Shift key and log in as usual.

To verify that macOS protections are active, open the Mac System Preferences, select "Security and Privacy" and click the General tab.

Now, check that Gatekeeper is active by checking that there is a check mark next to the App Store and identified developers.

If not, click on the padlock at the bottom of the page, enter your account password and tick the box.

Finally, check that the Xprotect database updates are active.

Go to "System Preferences", then to the App Store and check the box next to "Install system data files and security updates".

Robert M. Huss
Cybersecurity and Hacking

Glossary

Antispam: programs and filters that can select and discard emails that contain malware, advertising, etc.

Backup: copy the data contained in your device.

Banner: box that contains a simple advertising message but that can contain a malicious file that infects the computer if it is displayed.

Botnet: A set of computers infected with malware that allows the cracker to use them to decrypt passwords.

Cloud: A set of technologies that allow computer resources to be used through the Internet connection.

USB Controller: a device that can interface the computer with external devices connected via a USB port.

Cracker: The bad hacker who uses his computer skills for criminal purposes.

Data Recovery: A set of procedures put in place to recover data contained in corrupted devices.

Exploit: indicates the set of actions to be performed to take control of an information system starting from its venerability.

Framework: is the set of software modules that integrate with the operating system and make all the common functions available to the applications.

Hacker: this is the person with computer skills that allow him to enter a system and check its vulnerability. Often, after discovering the vulnerability of a system, the hacker communicates his discoveries to the programmers and suggests the solution of the problem.

Honeypot: it is a site or a computer network that acts as a trap for those who try to break into a computer system.

Hotspot: the access point to a Wi-Fi network.

HTML: is the language used to give shape to texts on websites.

IP address: represents the identification number of each device connected to a network. This numeric code can be 32 (IPv4) bits or 128 (IPv6) bits.

Javascript: programming language used to create interactive applications on the web.

Keygen: is a serial code generator used to install pirated software. Crackers to carry viruses often use these serial code generators. In fact, the keygen asks permission to access computer files. Once permission has been obtained, the keygen can modify what it wants.

Keylogger: is a type of virus that is installed on the computer, records everything that is typed on the keyboard and transmits it to the cracker.

Malware: any type of software that can enter a computer illegally and compromise its operation.

P2P: is a set of services that allows you to illegally exchange protected files using various protocols.

Patch: is a software package that contains codes to update the related software. The update lets you fix errors, remove vulnerabilities and optimize performance.

Payload: is that part of the malware that implements the cracker's criminal intentions. This happens after the exploit takes possession of the computer.

Plug-in: is a module of a more complex software that adds functions not initially foreseen.

Ransomware: is the most dangerous malware. It is able to encrypt all the data on the computer and ask for a ransom in exchange for the encryption key. Finally, it is able to infect all computers connected to the network.

Registry: it is the Windows file that contains the settings that regulate the operation of the operating system.

Spyware: is a type of software that collects information about a user's online activity without his or her consent.

Social Engineering: A set of techniques used by crackers to obtain information from people through the manipulation of their good faith.

Trojan Horse: is a type of malware disguised as a data file. Its characteristic is that it must have permission to install itself.

Virus: is a type of malware that can self-install itself and replicate itself by infecting other computers as well.

VPN: is a service that allows you to use the Internet as if it were a private network.

Wi-Fi: is the technology of wireless communication between computers and peripheral devices located within a short distance. With the help of the router, the local Wi-Fi network is able to connect to the Internet.

Worm: is a particular category of malware that can replicate itself.

Zero day: this is the security flaw in a software discovered by crackers but unknown to programmers.

Robert M. Huss
Cybersecurity and Hacking

HACKING

By

Robert M. Huss

Robert M. Huss
Cybersecurity and Hacking

DEFINITIONS

Computer Security: It is the protection of the computer systems of a public or private company through the use of products, services, organizational rules and individual behaviors that aim to protect the network from external attacks. The task of information security is to protect sensitive data from unwanted access, ensure the functioning of services, and guarantee the confidentiality of information in the face of unexpected events.

The objective is to protect and store information with the same care with which one takes care of one's own precious personal effects such as jewelers deposited in the bank. The computer system is the safe of our information; computer security is the same as the locks, combinations and keys used to protect it.

Hacking is the set of methods, techniques and operations put in place by a person (hacker) with the aim of knowing, entering and modifying a computer hardware or software system.

Hacking refers more generally to the solution of a problem through the use of creativity, not only in relation to computer science.

Robert M. Huss
Cybersecurity and Hacking

CHAPTER 1   Types of Hacking

Typical hacking activities are divided into types and objectives.

Increased performance (hardware). You can alter the operation of the physical circuits of a computer in order to achieve an increase in performance. In practice, improvements are made, not yet tested, to improve performance. For example, forcing a CD burner to work at twice the speed by removing a resistor. Other examples concern some personal computer motherboards on which, by modifying the connectors, it is possible to alter the frequency parameters of the installed processor, making it work at greater performance. This last practice is called overclocking (in modern motherboards the connectors called jumpers have been replaced by special BIOS software functions that can also be altered).

Removal of operating limitations: The use of electronic components (hardware) or applications (software) may be restricted in specific situations, as manufacturers have added internal functions to their products that restrict their use. The task of hacking is to circumvent these limitations. Sometimes, this action can be illegal. For example, to circumvent the purchase of licenses (hacking).

Altering the structure of a program: A software is structured on a sequence of operations to be performed by the computer on which it is installed; if the programs are "open source" this sequence of operations is made known and is also freely alterable, however, there is no possibility of intervention in protected software. In this case, the hacker intervenes on the software to modify it and bring it to execute the sequence of operations in a different way from the one chosen by the manufacturer, thus obtaining the "jump" (i.e. the non-execution) of some operations; this is called crack. Cracking a program means altering the structure of the software, causing the jump in operations that should verify the originality of the license. This practice can make it illegal to use the software even if it is legally purchased.

Adding functions to a program: Even the addition of new functions in a software is not allowed, but technically this operation is generally possible. This practice can make it illegal to use the software even if it is legally purchased.

Public communication network: Telecommunications networks have rules governing their use by each user. However, with access to a point in the network, it is possible to access and use the network without authorization. One of the most famous cases was that of being able to make free intercontinental calls using a blue box from anywhere on the telephone network, a device that, simulating the "tones" of service between operators in different countries, allowed the opening of unforeseen channels and therefore not subject to charging; this practice is known as phreaking.

Publication of unauthorized content on the Web: This case consists of pretending to be an authorized user to use another's computer, so it can attack a web server and alter the information stored on it. This practice is commonly called defacing. This practice has helped to make hacking famous, also attracting the curiosity of non-IT experts. We always remember that this practice can violate laws and privacy.

Private communication network: the unauthorized use of a local area computer (LAN) network is the same as in the previous case; it differs only in the size of the target, which in the case of a private network is more restricted. This practice has been facilitated by the spread of wireless networks. This practice of unauthorized use of private networks is called "wardriving". Remember that this practice violates the laws governing telecommunications and privacy.

Private communications network with unauthorized access: In this case, gaps in the security system controlling access to the networks are exploited. This case is referred to as hacking. Social engineering is the technique that exploits one of the security vulnerabilities of every computer system: the user. This practice may violate applicable laws.

CHAPTER 2　　　The Path of a Hacker

The hacker is a specialist in digital security. The prerequisite for becoming a hacker is computer competence. Becoming a hacker is the aspiration of many young fans of the Internet and electronic devices. The figure of the hacker arouses a lot of curiosity in today's young people, who find themselves wondering how to become a hacker.

Before we explain to you what is the path to take and the basic knowledge to know to become a hacker, let us define what is a hacker and how to become one.

What is a hacker?

The hacker is a computer expert who, thanks to his deep knowledge, is able to access a computer, a network, a protected account without being authorized. The hacker, therefore, commits a violation. However, one must distinguish between hackers ("good") and crakers ("bad"). Hackers generally get into other people's systems and devices to snoop around and test their skills, or to make their computer systems protected and unassailable. Access to another's network or computer without authorization is a crime. Professional hackers do not use their skills to commit illegal or illicit acts that undermine and damage the security of others, such as stealing sensitive data, theft or damaging systems by creating viruses.

How to become a Hacker

The figure of the hacker is undoubtedly one of those that most attracts young people today. The basic requirement to become a hacker is a passion for computer networks, programming languages and everything related to the Internet.

Today in the age of computer science, even if it is mainly young people who are attracted by becoming hackers, it must be said that there are no age limits to be a professional hacker. Anyone who is suited to computer science and is able to solve problems and find solutions can become an expert in computer systems. There are also those who become professional hackers after having completed a long process of studies and practical experience.

Which are the requirements

The aspiring hacker, before entering "illegally" into the networks and devices of others must know how to do. Those who have a strong passion and curiosity for the world of the Internet, computer networks, virtual data and computer security should first choose a course of study that directs them towards this sector.

These are the main requirements:

> The necessary but not sufficient condition to become a real hacker is to learn what is a computer and how it is make and obviously to learn how to use the computer.

> Learn a programming language. Learning a programming language allows you to understand what a computer is and how it is make. It is advisable to learn a simple language like Python and then move on to more complicated languages like C++, HTML, Java, PHP, SQL. For this, you can make use of manuals that you find both in the library and online that explain how to do, but also online tutorials that show you step by step how programming works. To start it is a good idea to use a good platform (Kali,

Backtrack 5 R3 or Ubuntu 12.04LTS). Also, learn how to use UNIX, the Internet's operating system. You cannot be a network hacker without understanding how the internet works.

➢ In-depth knowledge of the main operating systems (Windows, Linux and OS X) and command lines.

➢ Knowledge of hardware components and their operation.

➢ Train to create simple programs; it will help you to become familiar with the programming languages.

➢ It is essential to learn the basics of HTM to be able to make a simple home page and use it as a starting point.

➢ Learn to leave no trace. So learn how to become anonymous on the network.

➢ It is an excellent starting point to participate in events and conferences, turn to forums and blogs in the industry to receive support and exchange views on computer security. I remind you that "cracking" is an illegal activity that can lead to heavy penalties.

➢ Want to increase your multimedia culture: having a real curiosity to become the basis of programming and networks.

CHAPTER 3   The Hacking Process

The hacking process can last from a few days to several months, depending on the target and the risk.

The hacking process is structure in 5 basic steps.

Gathering information

As in all, the things we want to do but do not know we are looking for information on the subject. For example, when we go on holiday to a new destination, we try to inform ourselves by collecting as much information as possible.

Similarly, a hacker spends a lot of time gathering information on a site when he decides to "attack" it. An easy way to collect information is to Google information about it.

Through the use of simple commands, you can discover the IP address of the website and much more information.

With the **whois** command to which you add the site you want to know about (example, whois yhaoo.com), you can find out which internet provider has a specific IP address and information about the owner, registration date and expiration date of a domain.

With the command **nslookup** + website address, you can get from a domain its IP address or host name and vice versa.

You need to be well informed and know things in detail because otherwise you risk your freedom.

Scanning

Once the target information is collected, a hacker needs to have information that is more technical. With tools such as Nmap, you can scan networks and servers, to make a mapping of the network or server you want to attack. Therefore, you have specific information about the type of network, the operating system used, the equipment used and much more. After obtaining this information (e.g. the operating system used) the hacker can search the Internet for vulnerabilities of the operating system to be attack. At this point, the hacker can move on to the third phase.

Getting Access

Once all possible information has been collect, the hacker can move on to the attack phase. The attack must be designed so as not to generate alarms. The main tools used to generate a cyber-attack are SQL, Burp suite, Metasploit and so on. It all depends on the goal you want to achieve and the technology used.

Access can be do in several ways:

- Access to a final device of a network (tablet, smarpkone, pc, etc.).
- Access to the control panel of a website.
- Root access on a Linux server.
- Access to a certain equipment (firewall, router, etc.).

Once entered the network, the hacker can get all the possible information.

Maintaining access

At this stage, the hacker must create the conditions to maintain access. That is, it must leave the doors open to return to the system. These ports are calls "backdoors". The software developers themselves often create these access points. In this way, the hacker can easily enter and exit without anyone noticing. The information a hacker collects is usually sold on the black market (Deep Web).

We reiterate that unauthorized access to a system leads to serious criminal prosecution.

At this stage, the hacker has to worry about hiding the traces. To do this they need to know how the technology works.

It is very important to know how the server you want to access works.

It is also important to know how the Windows and Linux operating systems work. It is important to know where the user's access data is stored. How users are creates. Where their data is stored. What happens when you access the operating system and more.

Finally, to leave no trace of your location you need to use the VPN and/or Tor services for encryption and traffic anonymity.

Once you leave the system, you must delete all tracks. Therefore, you have to delete all the logs from the different applications. Delete user logs and delete all logs from all different monitoring systems.

To do this you do not need to search for individual files, but you can use programs such as ntsecurity .nu, on windows that do all the work.

If the operating system is Linux, you can use the following commands:

#rm ./bash_history to delete the current user's data

#vim/ var/log/messages that is used to delete the logs that have been generate.

What is Ethical Hacking?

A white hat hacker is a computer enthusiast, programming expert, systems and computer security expert who can break into computer networks in order to help owners become aware of a security problem in their network. White hackers are opposed to black haters, those who illegally violate computer systems, even without personal advantage.

Ethical hacking refers to the action of testing controlled intrusions into computer systems.

The Ethical Hacker is a professional increasingly sought after by companies around the world because of its unique skills in computer security.

Moreover, the hacker, in studying software and hardware, often tries to disassemble and reassemble the same, in an attempt to improve them or to have new results, reaching a deeper and deeper knowledge of these systems.

CHAPTER 4   Installing and Using Kali Linux

What is Kali Linux?

Kali Linux is a distribution based on Debian and is designed for computer security and forensic computing, in particular to perform penetration tests, which are essential to test the security of networks and computer systems. It is create and managed by the Offensive Security group. It is considered the successor of Backtrack. The update of the distribution is rolling.

Today Kali Linux is one of the best tools for experts in computer and network security. In fact, it offers all the tools needed to monitor and perform security tests on any type of network or computer system.

Heir to the famous BackTrack, in recent years is increasingly used by experts in the field and not, thanks to frequent updates and bug fixes.

Kali offers users access to a large collection of tools for security from port scanning to password crackers. Its GUI is GNOME 3 but there are other versions with KDE, MATE, Xfce or LXDE. It supports live CD and live USB, this feature offers users booting Kali directly from CD/USB without the need for installation, although in the options there is the possibility of installation on the hard disk. This means that it can be booted on most computers, being mobile, but also that it "leaves no trace" of its use, ideal for performing security tests without installing anything on the host computer. It is a supported platform for the Metasploit Project framework, a tool for developing and executing exploits to remote machines or to machines belonging to your LAN. It also contains security programs: Wireshark, John the Ripper, Nmap and Aircrack-ng.

Features of Kali Linux

Currently Kali Linux has over 350 dedicated tools for each different type of use, including information gathering, vulnerability analysis, password cracking, network analysis, wireless hacking, reporting tools, hardware hacking, forensic tools, stress testing and a set of exploitation tools.

As we mentioned, Kali Linux is based on Debian from which it inherits stability and security, but uses independent repositories. This allows the Kali team to keep the various packages up to date with the latest versions.

Kali Linux is multilingual and fully customizable. You can create a custom version with your own preferences and graphical settings. The kernel is patched for Wi-Fi injection, runs on a wide variety of hardware, and supports many wireless devices, both USB and other.

Processor Support:

- Armel
- Armhf
- i386, x86_64
- Kali is currently available for the following ARM devices:
- k3306 mk/ss808
- Raspberry Pi
- ODROID U2/X2
- Samsung Chromebook

In the latest versions, Kali provides several desktops such as Gnome, XFCE, LXDE, and Mate.

Among the most useful tools that come with Kali Linux

➢ **Wireshark.** This is a real-time traffic analysis tool. All traffic on a network node is broken down into useful packet metadata, including header, routing information, and payload. It is a protocol analysis software used for network problem solving, protocol analysis and development or communication software. This tool can be used to detect and analyze network security and to solve network problems.

➢ **Mestasploit Framework.** Metasploit is a computer security project that provides information about vulnerabilities simplify penetration testing operations and helps in the development of intrusion detection systems. The most well-known sub-project is Metasploit Framework, an open source tool for the development and execution of exploits against a remote machine. It has a number of options for the user interface and provides the ability to attack almost any operating system.

➢ **Nmap.** Abbreviation for network map, it is a common but indispensable tool for penetration testing. It is free software distributed under the GNU GPL by Insecure.org and designed to detect open ports on a target computer or even on IP address ranges, to determine which network services are available. It can guess which operating system the target computer is using.

➤ **John de ripper**. It is a free software tool for cracking passwords. It can decrypt passwords encrypted in DES, MD5 and Blowfish. With the addition of additional modules that extend its capacity, they have also allowed the decryption of MD4 systems in LDAP and MySQL. One of the most useful features of this tool is the ability to automatically detect the type of encryption "hash" of passwords. There is also a commercial version of this tool that supports the cracking of many more hash password algorithms.

➤ **Aircrack-ng**. This tool is equipped with features for wireless network analysis, packet injection and encryption of password cracking tools. It requires a network interface hardware that supports monitor functionality.

This list is obviously not complete, but only represents a sample of the power and flexibility that Kali Linux provides as a platform for penetration testing and computer security in general.

How to install Kali Linux

Kali Linux, as mentioned above, is a Debian-based Linux distribution full of tools dedicated to penetration testing and forensic computing, already configured and ready to use.

In this chapter, we will talk about the various versions of Kali Linux and how to install them on a USB stick, how to run them in live mode and how to make a real installation of the operating system on your computer. The process is not difficult just a little 'patience and a few minutes of free time.

Minimum requirements for various versions of Kali Linux

Kali Linux is a Linux distribution designed primarily for testing network security. It is available for both 32-bit and 64-bit computers and is equipped with a series of programs designed for this purpose. It can be downloaded with or without a desktop environment.

The available versions are as follows:

- ➢ **Basic version**: it is equipped with the Gnome3 desktop environment.
- ➢ **E17**: includes the desktop Enlightenment version E17 and all the software for security.
- ➢ **KDE**: This version represents a variant of the operating system equipped with KDE Plasma environment.
- ➢ **Mate:** This version is equipped with the Mate desktop environment.
- ➢ **XFCE:** equipped with the Xfce decktop environment.
- ➢ **Light:** This version has no pre-installed desktop environment. In addition, the ISO image is smaller than the others are, and you can add a desktop environment later, using the Internet connection. It is recommended for experienced users or server systems.
- ➢ **Virtualbox and VMware**: are files that allow you to view your operating system in a few clicks using the Virtualbox and VMware software.

Today, Kali Linux can be easily installed on the hard disk of your computer, using a simple graphical procedure.

Instead, initially, Kali Linux is design as a distribution to be booted via USB stick and without leaving traces on the disk at the next reboot. If necessary, there is the possibility to save the modified files on the USB stick itself, for reuse at the next reboot.

In all cases, the minimum requirements for running Kali Linux are:

- 1 GB of RAM.
- In the case of disk installation, a partition with at least 20 GB of space.
- To install it on a machine (physical or virtual), it is recommended to have at least 2 or more GB of RAM. This results in a stable desktop system that does not crash.

Installation on a USB key

To boot Kali Linux from USB, you need to create a USB stick and have your computer boot from it from the operating system image.

Start by downloading the most suitable version of Kali Linux for you from the official website. Click on the HTTP button located at the version of Kali Linux you have chosen and start the download. I will refer to the basic version of Kali Linux 64 bit.

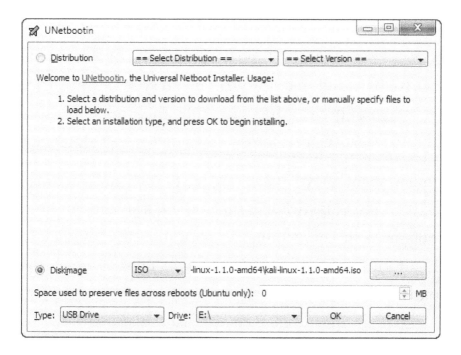

Now download the Unetbootin program from this page by clicking on the button most suitable for the operating system you are using, for example download (Windows) if you are using Windows, and then connect the USB stick on which you intend to install Kali Linux to your computer.

Once this operation is complete, start the program you just downloaded by pressing the Yes button and, in the proposed window, place a check mark next to the Disk image item.

If you are using a Mac, start the program by copying it to the Applications folder and type in your administrator password.

Now, make sure that the Type drop-down menu selects the USB Drive item and that the Drive menu specifies the drive letter of your drive. After checking this, press the "..." button to select the previously downloaded Kali Linux ISO.

As mentioned above, you can save files and settings directly to the USB stick and make them available for later reboots, as Kali Linux supports persistent boot mode. To take advantage of this possibility, you must indicate the amount of space to devote to these files (in MB), acting on the text field Space reserved for user files that will be protected from various reboots.

Once the settings are complete, press the OK button and wait for the creation process to be completed.

Once you have created your drive, boot from it and set your computer's BIOS to boot directly from USB.

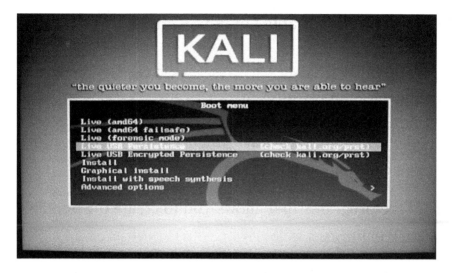

When the operating system finishes the boot procedure, a screen of choice is displayed. Select Live (amd64) or Live USB Persistence, which allows you to save files and settings directly to the USB stick. This way the operating system is completely run from the USB stick and leaves no trace on the computer's hard drive.

Once you have completed the system initialization sequence, you can use Kali Linux with the confidence that whatever you do will not affect your computer's disk. As for access, the pre-configured root user password is "toor": you can use it if you need it to run the onboard software.

How to create a bootable Linux USB stick

Creating a bootable USB stick is quite easy to do.

To create a bootable USB stick you need to use applications that you can find free on the internet.

One of the programs that allows you to create the bootable USB stick is Rufus.

This program only works on Windows, but allows you to create USB sticks with all Linux distributions, including Ubuntu, from the ISO files that can be downloaded from the official websites of the latter.

Another program that allows you to create the bootable USB is UNetbootin.

This program is available not only for Windows, but also for macOS and Linux. It also allows you to directly download the installation files for the different Linux distributions, without the need to download the ISO files in advance.

After you have logged in to the UNetbootin website, download it to your computer. Start by pressing the download button for the operating system you are using on the PC you are going to use to create the bootable USB stick. Once the download is complete, start UNetbootin (the program does not need to be installed on Windows, while it must be copied in the Applications folder on macOS), answer Yes to the warning that appears on the screen (or type the password of your user account if you use a Mac), put a check mark next to the Distribution item and choose the operating system to download (es. Ubuntu) from the drop-down menu.

Finally, select the drive of the USB stick from the "Type" drop-down menu, press the OK button and wait for your USB stick to be create with Linux.

At the end of the procedure, boot from the USB stick and proceed to the installation or live execution of Linux, following the instructions on the screen. If you cannot boot from the key for installing Linux, you may need to disable the secure boot, enable legacy BIOS mode in your PC's UEFI settings and/or change some boot files on the key.

Installation on a PC

Kali Linux can be install on a PC in two ways: on disk or by creating a virtual machine.

On disk

The first step is to create a bootable USB stick with Kali Linux using Unetbootin. Once this operation is completed, create two partitions on the hard disk of your computer to contain Kali Linux: the one on which the operating system is installed must be at least 20 GB, while the second, called swap, must be equal to twice the RAM on the PC.

Once the disk configuration procedure is complete, restart the computer by booting from USB and once you have access to the menu of choice of Kali Linux, select the item Graphical Install using the arrow keys of the keyboard, then press the Enter key.

Now, proceed according to the on-screen installation instructions: select your language, click the Continue button, select your country, click the Continue button, choose your keyboard from the list, click the Continue button again and wait for the components needed for the installation to load.

Next, type your computer name in the Host Name text box, press the Continue button, and repeat the operation for the domain name.

Now, you will need to create a password that you will need to access your root account if you need to: type the password in both proposed boxes and click the Continue button.

If you have, an entire disk at your disposal, select the Guided entry and in this way the entire disk will be used and everything on the disk will be delete. Tap on Continue and select the chosen disc from the next screen.

If, on the other hand, you have created partitions manually, select Manual and click on Continue, select the partition that your operating system should contain, press on Continue, and follow the on-screen instructions to set the mount / point on it.

Repeat the operation also for the swap partition and select the Finish partitioning item, write the changes to the disk and click the Continue button, select the Yes box and press the Continue button again. This will delete all data irreversibly present.

Wait for the installation to finish and check the Yes box and press the Continue button twice to configure future package updates and installations.

At this point, you need to install a small program that allows you to choose the operating system to boot, after installing the boot loader, select Yes, press the Continue button, select the main hard drive (the one on which the existing operating system is installed) and click the Continue button again.

Once the installation is finished, press on "Continue", wait for the computer to restart. Choose Kali Linux from the GRUB menu to use the operating system now.

On virtual machine

Kali Linux can be install on a virtual machine, but first you need to perform a long virtual installation procedure that requires time and skills.

To overcome this, Kali Linux provides virtual applications that contain entire installations of Kali Linux and that can be easily added to programs such as Virtualbox in a few minutes.

Start downloading the VirtualBox manager from its download page, choosing the version best suited to your operating system, then start the downloaded file and finish the setup by following the simple on-screen instructions.

Once VirtualBox is installed, connect to the Kali Linux virtual applications Internet page, scroll down to locate the Kali Linux VirtualBox Images section, select it with a click, and press the 32-bit or 64-bit version of the operating system (e.g. Kali-Linux VBox 64-Bit [OVA]) to download the application.

After completing the download, double-click the file you just downloaded, if necessary select VirtualBox Manager from the list of proposed applications, press the Import button attached to the new window shown on the screen.

Once the import procedure is finished, select the virtual machine you just created from the side panel of the

VirtualBox start screen, press the Start button at the top. Once you have reached the login screen, type in the root user name followed by the Enter button, and repeat the operation with the "toor" password.

At this point, you can use Kali Linux and customize it as you wish. You can change the language settings (by pressing the "settings" button and then "region & language"), you can change the keyboard layout (by pressing the "+" button, located below the "input source" box). You can create an administrator user in order to avoid root access: to do so, press on the system indicator at the top right, then on the root and "Account settings" items.

Press the "Add User" button in the upper right corner of the new window, click the "Administrator" button, fill in the forms with the required information, move the check mark next to the "Set a password now" entry and press the "Add" button.

How to set up Kali Linux on Windows 10

If you use Windows 10, you do not need to install Kali Linux on disk or create virtual machines because you can install it inside the Windows operating system.

In fact, thanks to the Linux subsystem made available within Windows 10, you can download and install Kali Linux from the Microsoft Store, and use it via the Command Prompt.

The first step will be to activate the Linux subsystem. Open the Start menu and type the phrase "Windows functionality" in the search bar and click on the icon.

Identify on the new screen that appears on your desktop, the Windows Subsystem for Linux item, tick the corresponding box, press OK and then click the "Restart now" button to make the required change effective.

Now, connect to the Windows Store, type Kali Linux in the search bar, search, select the operating system icon from the results and press the Get button to install it immediately.

Once the installation is complete, start Kali Linux from the start menu, clicking on its icon and wait for the completion of the operating system setup: when Enter new UNIX username appears, choose a username, press the Enter key, enter the access password, press the Enter key and repeat the operation to confirm the password. Kali Linux is finally install.

Before proceeding with any further steps, it is advisable to type the command "sudo apt-get update && sudo apt-get dist-upgrade" to perform a complete system update.

To use a desktop with a mouse and keyboard, you will need to install a graphical interface, using Xfce on Kali Linux and the remote Windows desktop. If this will result in sudden malfunctions and blockages of Linux, simply restart the computer.

Once logged into Kali Linux, type in the command "sudo apt-get install wget", press the Enter button twice, then enter the command "wget https://kali.sh/xfce4.sh" and press Enter again. At this point, type the command "sudo sh xfce4.sh" and press Enter, type your administrator password and press Enter again: after a few minutes, the configuration process will start.

Using the keyboard's directional arrows, configure the keyboard mapping: select "Other" from the list, press the Enter button, choose your language (e.g. English), press Enter again, select your language again from the next window and always press Enter.

Once the procedure is complete, the phrase Configuring XRDP to listen on port 3390 (but not starting the service) is shown on the screen, then type the command "sudo /etc/init.d/xrdp start" followed by Enter, type your administrator password, press Enter and make sure the service is started on port 3390 (a green "ok" is shown on the screen).

At this point, keeping the Kali Linux command window open, open the Windows Start menu, type the phrase "Remote Desktop" in the search bar, click the Remote Desktop Connection icon, enter the string "localhost: 3390" in the Computer box, then press "Connect", check the box "Do not display this message again" for connections to this computer and press the Yes button.

Now, on the Kali Linux GUI, all you have to do is type your username and password in the fields provided and click OK, taking care to leave the Xorg entry in the Session field.

Before closing the Remote Desktop window, log out of the session by clicking on your username at the top right.

Working with Kali Linux

Starting from the desktop of Kali Linux, you will have on the left a bar with some tools but above all, you can see the terminal.

By clicking on the menu "applications" in the upper left corner have the pen testing that we can use.

These applications are hacking programs that can be used with both good and bad intentions. It all depends on you whether you want to become a white hacker or a black hacker.

These tools help us to get more information about our target audience.

Once you have clicked on one of these programs, it may happen that:

- The program opens with the GUI interface.

- A terminal is running and displays its information.

In the first case, it can be intuitive what to do. In the second case, you will open a program with a kind of help menu. In both cases, it is important to understand how that program works.

Example: Yersinia is a graphical tool that allows you to launch MITM attacks. There is another version that starts with the command #Yersinia -G. This Yersinia GUI version is more powerful and customizable.

This is just a brief introduction to Kali Linux.

CHAPTER 5   How to Scan the Network and Servers

In this chapter, we will talk about scanning networks and servers with a few commands on Kali Linux and a few clicks on windows.

Scanning a network means finding out what devices are connected to the network, what types of devices, what is the operating system and its version, what ports to open, what applications are running on those ports. To do this, we will refer to the Nmap program.

Once we have collected all this information, we can understand how the network is structured, test the network and servers and analyze their vulnerability in an ethical way.

Scanning a network with Nmap

This program is among the most used by hackers and ethical hackers. Nmap is an easy to use, free tool and helps us map the network with an easy to understand output. On Windows the interface is called Zenmap.

Here are some commands:

- #nmap -sP 192.168.1.0/24: this allows us to see the number of devices on the network.
- #nmap -sS 192.168.1.0/24: This allows us to discover the open ports on each device.
- #nmap -A 192.168.1.1: This command allows us to scan every single device on the network to discover the open ports and operating system used.
- #nmap -sT 192.168.1.254: This command scans using TCP packets.
- #nmap -uU 192.168.1.1: This scans using UDP packets.
- #nmap -F 192.168.1.0/24: This command scans for the most commonly used ports.
- #nmap -sS-p 80,443,23,22,25 192.168.1.1: This command scans for ports found with -p using TCP SYN packets.
- #nmap -F -oN rezultat_scanare.txt 192.168.1.0/24: this command stores the result on results.txt file, useful for a Python script.

If you want to get more information about the scan, in real time, you can add -v to any type of command.

Scanning with Hping3

This is another tool that we can use together with Nmap. Hping3 is a traffic generator that is able to send TCP, UDP or RAW-IP packets.

Hping3 allows us to do:

- Firewall testing
- MTU detection on manual route
- Checking TCP/IP batteries
- Taking fingerprints of the operating system.
- Network testing using different TOS protocols.
- Guess remote uptime
- Advanced scanning.

Here are some commands:

- ✓ #hping3 -h: this command allows you to have more information about the available topics
- ✓ #hping3 -1 VICTIM_IP: A normal ping is sent.
- ✓ #hping3 -traceroute -V -1 VICTIM_IP: only one packet of paths is sent.

- ✓ #hping3 -V -S -p 80 VICTIM_IP: in this case, the packets are sent to port 80 to check if the application responds.
- ✓ #hping3 -c 1 -V -p 80-s 5050-A VICTIM_IP: This command allows us to understand if a device is on the network when it does not respond to ping. It is possible that it is blocked by a firewall.
- ✓ #hping3 -c 1 -V -p 80 -s 5050 -A --rand-source VICTIM_IP: This command covers all traces, so no one can know where the scan came from.
- ✓ #hping3 -V -c 2000000 -d 100 -S -w 64 -p 443 -s 591 --flood --rand-source VICTIM_IP: In this command there are several arguments, for example:
  - o --flood, send packets faster
  - o -V, offers more information
  - o -c --count, indicates the number of packages
  - o --rand-source, generates the IP address
  - o --s--baseport, source port
  - o -w--win, window size
  - o -d--data, package size

Hping3 can also be used to make Dos attacks.

The most important thing is to know how the technology works. It is important to know the computer networks, the OSI model, the ports, the TCP protocol etc.

Network scanning is very important because it provides us with all the information we need to perform the penetration test.

We remind you that the penetration test is divided into 5 steps:

1. Collection of information
2. Scanning
3. Network or server access
4. Maintaining network or server access
5. Covering the tracks

To these 5 steps we add a sixth phase, that of ethical hacking.

Robert M. Huss
Cybersecurity and Hacking

CHAPTER 6   How to Hack a PC and How to Protect Yourself

We remind you that entering the computer systems of users and companies without having received the authorization can be a crime. We reiterate to use the information contained in this chapter only to verify the vulnerabilities of networks and improve their security. We recommend that you use this information with ethical hacking.

Tools for hacking the PC

One of the main tools used to hack your pc is known as the **Backdoor**.

With this tool, the black hacker can act remotely by taking control of the pc. In this way, the black hacker could install malicious software on the victim's computer or use the victim's computer to convey other cyber-attacks. In fact, once the communication bridge between him and the victim's computer is created, without the victim noticing anything, the black hacker can act undisturbed.

The black hacker is able to create these communication bridges thanks to software called **trojans**. This software is sent by email through infected links or by having the victim download apparently innocent software.

Another tool used by cybercriminals is the **Keylogger**. This tool installs itself in the victim's system, records everything that is typed on the keyboard and sends this information to the black hacker. In this way, the cybercriminal becomes aware of the victim's password and sensitive data.

Keyloggers, besides being in the form of software, can also be built as physical devices. In this case, they can be placed between the keyboard and the computer and record everything that is typed.

Another tool used by black hackers to approach the designated victim and with an excuse to ask permission to use the computer. In this case, the cybercriminal installs spy software on the victim's computer.

More than a tool, it can be defined as a tactic used by the black hacker, called social engineering.

How to protect your PC

The first thing to do to protect your PC is to install an anti-virus that can monitor your computer and block any malicious software.

In the latest versions of windows, is included an anti-malware, Windows Defender. In addition, you can download from the internet a number of free anti-virus and anti-malware such as Bitdefender, Avast, Avira, Malwarebytes Anti-Malware

Although Macs are less vulnerable to external attacks, excellent anti-malware such as "Malwarebytes for Mac" and "Bitdefender Antivirus Scanner" are available.

Another tool you can use to defend your computer from hackers is the Firewall.

The Firewall is a perimeter defense component of a computer network, which can also act as a link between two or more network segments, providing protection in terms of computer security of the network itself.

The Windows and macOS operating systems already have an integrated and active firewall by default.

This firewall integrated into the operating system can be upgraded with other tools such as: Windows Firewall Control for Windows and Little Snitch for macOS.

The firewall can be either software or hardware.

To prevent possible cyber-attacks, it is advisable to avoid downloading software from dubious sources. It is preferable to download programs from Microsoft and Apple stores, because inside the stores, the programs go through a long process of analysis and review, before being available for download.

If you download programs outside the stores, it is advisable to check their reliability before downloading them using online tools such as VirtusTotal and Wot.

Another way to prevent attacks is not to open attachments received by email.

Many web programs and services for accessing e-mails block the reception of executable files from the operating system. Specifically, these files have extensions such as: .exe, .java, .dmg, .vba, .js. However, you should also pay attention to other types of files such as PDF and Office files.

Avoid using public Wi-Fi networks, as they are not adequately protected, they are very vulnerable to cyber-attacks and are often used by black hackers to capture data from users who are connected to them.

Finally, it is advisable to keep your operating system and the programs you use on your computer up to date. Updates often contain corrections to security holes that cybercriminals exploit to hack PCs.

Robert M. Huss
Cybersecurity and Hacking

www.ingramcontent.com/pod-product-compliance
Lightning Source LLC
Chambersburg PA
CBHW071550080326
40690CB00056B/1627